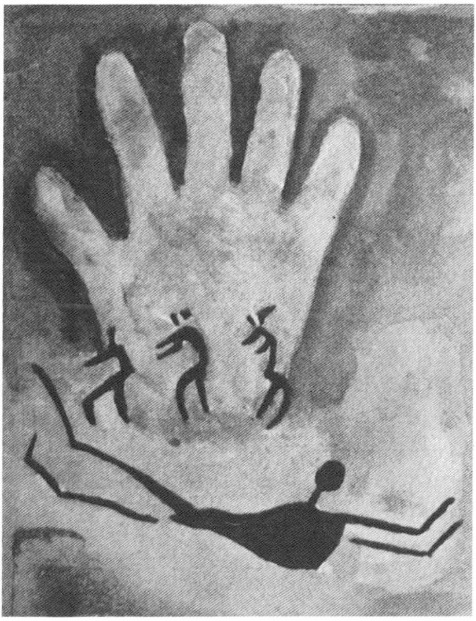

GILF KEBIR NATIONAL PARK

Alberto Siliotti

GEODIA EDIZIONI

Wadi Hamra (Gilf Kebir)

Text and Photos Alberto Siliotti
Drawings Stefania Cossu
English Translation Richard Pierce
Editorial Director Yvonne Marzoni
Graphic Design Geodia

The text of the chapter *Flora* is by Frank Darius.
The text of the box *11 May 2002: the Discovery* is by Massimo Foggini.

ISBN 978 88 87177 84 8 Dar el-Kutub 17614/2009

The Author

For over twenty years, journalist and writer Alberto Siliotti has studied the history, culture and natural environment of Egypt. A member of the Egypt Exploration Society and the Egyptian Geographical Society, he has participated in many scientific missions and has curated important exhibitions. Siliotti is the author of very popular books and guides that have been translated into many languages. These include Nefertari and the Valley of the Queens *(1993),* Egypt: Temples, Men and Gods *(1994, 2004),* Guide to the Exploration of Sinai *(1994, 2003),* Guide to the Valley of the Kings and the Theban Necropolises and Temples *(1996, 2004),* Guide to the Pyramids of Egypt *(1997, 2003),* The Discovery of Ancient Egypt *(1998),* Dwellings of Eternity *(2000),* Belzoni's Travels *(2001),* Hidden Treasures of Antiquity *(2006), the collection* Egypt Pocket Guides *(2000, 2002, 2003, 2007),* St. Catherine, the Monastery and its Territory *(2008), the* Map of the Western Desert: Oases of Egypt *(2007, 2009), the* Map of White Desert National Park *(2008), the* Map of Gilf Kebir National Park *(2009). For ten years he has been engaged in the study of the Western Desert in Egypt, and since 2002 has collaborated actively with the Egyptian Environment Affairs Agency and Italian Cooperation.*

Front Cover: *Wadi Hamra (Gilf Kebir)*
Title Page: *Wadi Sura. Watercolour by L. Almásy (1936)*

Contents

Neolithic paintings (Wadi Sura, Gilf Kebir)

Karkur Talh (Gebel Uweinat)

The dunes in the Great Sand Sea

A branch of Wadi Abd el-Malik (Gilf Kebir)

25°30′ N
25°00′ E
25°30′ N
26°00′ E
N
Silica
Glass
Area
Great Sand Sea
Signpost of the Park
Gilf Kebir Plateau
24°00′ N
26°40′ E
Abu Ras
Plateau
'The Gap'
Kamal el-Din
Plateau
Aqaba Pass
23°00′ N
26°40′ E
محمية الجلف الكبير
GILF KEBIR
NATIONAL PARK
Gebel
Uweinat
22°00′ N
25°30′ E
Gilf Kebir
National
Park

The Gilf Kebir National Park

This park is the largest of the 27 Protected Areas in Egypt and consists of three different geomorphic units: the Gilf Kebir Plateau proper, the Gebel Uweinat massif and the Great Sand Sea.

One of the large valleys in the Gilf Kebir park, the Wadi Abd el-Malik

On 4 January 2007, the Egyptian Prime Minister's Decree established the Gilf Kebir National Park (GKNP): it is adjacent to Libya to the west and borders Sudan to the south and with a total area of 48,533 square kilometers, is equal to five percent of Egyptian territory.

The ***Gilf Kebir Plateau*** is the heart of the park, a wide massif as large as two times the island of Corsica, dissected by immense valleys (or 'wadis'), which demonstrate that this region, now extremely arid, once abounded in water. Already about 10,500 years ago, numerous populations had settled here, leaving important traces of their presence, including splendid rock paintings that are a precious testimony of Saharan rock art.

Gebel Uweinat, which is situated about 150 km south of the Gilf Kebir Plateau and for the most part lies in Sudanese and Libyan territory, is another massif. It is 1,934 meters high and its geological formations are of extraordinary importance (indeed, the ancient crystalline basement is visible here), due to the presence of numerous plant species and the wealth of rock paintings and petroglyphs that decorate the wadis.

Lastly, the ***Great Sand Sea*** or *GSS* is a complex of sand dune chains, one of the largest and most impressive of its kind in the world, which extends for over 650 kilometers from the Siwa Oasis to the Gilf Kebir Plateau.

Between 2003 and 2004 it was proposed that the Gilf Kebir Plateau, Gebel Uweinat and some parts of the Great Sand Sea be included in the UNESCO World Heritage List.

The Geology

Multicolored sandstone

The rocks and formations in the Gilf Kebir National Park are testimony of a very ancient geological history that began hundreds of millions of years ago. Research into the geological features of the park will shed light on the past of our planet.

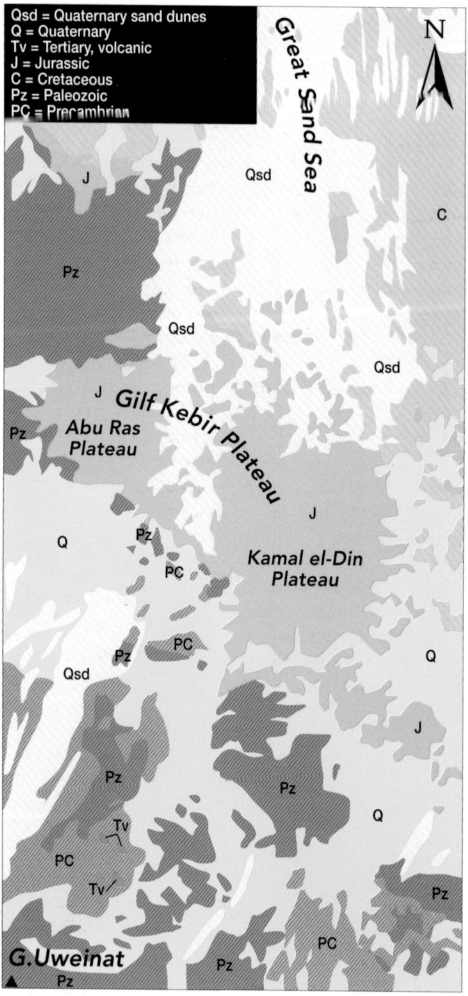

Simplified geological map of the Gilf Kebir National Park (from Egyptian Geological Survey, *1981, modified)*

The Gilf Kebir Plateau basically consists of Paleozoic sandstone covered with Jurassic-Cretaceous sandstone (the letter **J** in the geological map here at left), which was deposited when the entire region was submerged by the waters of a rather shallow tropical sea.

These rocks constitute the so-called Nubian sandstone formation that lies over the very ancient Precambrian (**PC**) crystalline basement that can easily be seen in the Gebel Uweinat area.

Nubian sandstone is easily recognizable by its color, which varies from light yellow to dark red and has a vast gamut of hues. It is bordered to the northwest and south by more ancient clastic formations dating to the Lower Paleozoic (**Pz**), and to the west by a broad band of much more recent formations dating to the Quaternary period (**Q**)—when the region had already emerged definitively—that are made up of either clayey and earthy deposits corresponding to beds of ancient lakes (the so-called *playa* lakes) or wadi deposits. Sometimes from among these formations there emerge very ancient Precambrian (**PC**) magmatic rocks (granite and granodiorites), as well as younger volcanic rocks such as basalt, trachyte and dolerite, which are easy to recognize because of their blackish color and which bear witness to the volcanic activity typical of the Tertiary period (**Tv**).

South of the Gilf Kebir Plateau, in the area lying between the plateau and Gebel Uweinat, traces of this activity are documented by the presence of ring dikes, for example the *Clayton Craters*.

Round granite typical of Gebel Uweinat

Outcrops of volcanic rocks (trachyte and basalt)

The western section of the Gebel Uweinat region is dominated by Precambrian granite, which forms a gigantic ring-shaped dike with a diameter of about twenty-four kilometers, the remains of a majestic intrusion eroded by atmospheric agents, while the eastern area consists of expanses of Paleozoic sandstone formations.

The most recent section of the GKNP formations in terms of geological time is the Great Sand Sea, which stretches over a huge area of 72,000 square kilometers (roughly the size of Ireland), only a small part of which is included in the protected area.

It is thought that the origin of this immense stretch of sand, which dates to the Quaternary period (**Qds**), a little less than two million years ago, was the erosive activity on pre-existing rocks of a massive river network that existed in the region at that time and that has been spotted in satellite images (Shuttle Imaging Radar or SIR).

The successive action of the wind then probably led to the formation of not only the huge mass of sand, but also of its configuration into chains of dunes.

Nubian sandstone often varies in color

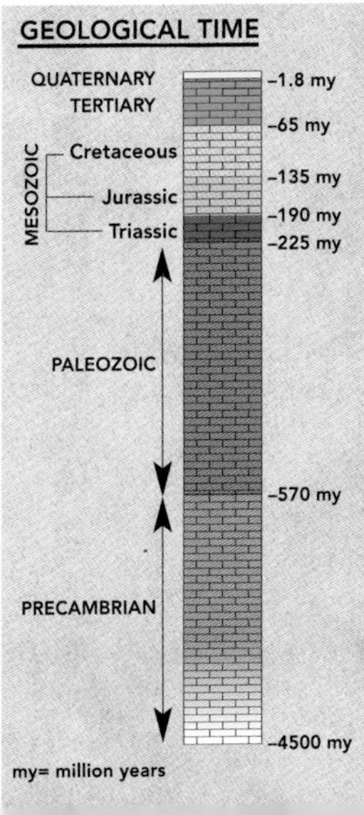

The Fauna

*The scimitar-horned oryx (*Oryx dammah*) and the addax (*Addax nasomaculatus*), which are now extinct*

Despite the extremely difficult climatic conditions, many animal species live in the Gilf Kebir National Park and their biodiversity is a source of continuous surprises.

It is quite surprising to note the level of adaptation of relatively abundant fauna to extreme and waterless environments such as those of the Gilf Kebir National Park.

The mammals there are represented above all by Barbary sheep (*Ammotragus lervia*), called *waddan* in Arabic, a species that in the prehistory period was widespread in the entire Sahara and even in the nineteenth century still lived throughout Egypt.

The Barbary sheep, which in the past was the victim of indiscriminate hunting, is now an endangered species that is quite rare, but some sheep survive in the Gilf Kebir, especially in the Abd el-Malik, Talh and Hamra wadis and in the upper parts of Gebel Uweinat, as well as in the Karkur Talh, all areas with vegetation that provides this creature with the necessary nourishment.

*The Barbary sheep (*Ammotragus lervia*) is an endangered species*

Another mammal that lives in the park area is the dorcas gazelle (*Gazella dorcas*), whose rare surviving individuals are concentrated for the most part in the valleys of Gebel Uweinat, while the scimitar-horned oryx (*Oryx dammah*) and the addax (*Addax nasomaculatus*), both of which can be seen in the prehistoric rock paintings and petroglyphs of this area, have become extinct: the last specimens of the addax in the region were spotted in the 1930s. Then there are the Rüppell's fox (*Vulpes rueppelli*)—the only carnivore in the entire area whose presence has been documented in both the Gilf Kebir and Uweinat—and above all such small rodents as the lesser Egyptian gerbil (*Gerbillus gerbillus*) and the lesser Egyptian jerboa (*Jaculus jaculus*), both of which are to found

*Rüppell's fox (*Vulpes rueppelli*)*

*The dorcas gazelle (*Gazella dorcas*)*

*The lesser Egyptian gerbil (*Gerbillus gerbillus*)*

The lesser Egyptian jerboa
(Jaculus jaculus)

everywhere in this territory.

As for the birds, the two species that reside in the park are the white wagtail (*Motacilla alba*) and the white-crowned wheatear (*Oenanthe leucopyga*), called *zarzur* in Arabic, which are widespread here.

The park area is also a

The white wagtail
(Motacilla alba)

The white-crowned wheatear
(Oenanthe leucopyga)

The hoopoe lark
(Alaemon alaudipes)

major passage point for numerous species of migratory birds. Among the ten species that build their nests here, almost all in the Uweinat zone, mention should be made of the sooty falcon (*Falco concolor*), the hoopoe-lark (*Alaemon alaudipes*), and the pharaoh eagle owl (*Bubo ascalaphus*).

Twelve species of reptiles have been

The red-spotted lizard
(Mesalina rubropunctata)

identified in the park. These include numerous lizards such as the Sinai blue agama (*Pseudotrapelus sinaitus*), the red-spotted lizard (*Mesalina rubropunctata*), and above all the sandfish (*Scincus scincus*), so named because it seems to be swimming when moving along the sand. The most common reptile is the Saharan sand snake (*Psammophis aegyptius*), which feeds mostly on small rodents.

Among the Lepidoptera, mention should be made of the painted lady (*Vanessa cardui*), a beautiful butterfly that can be seen

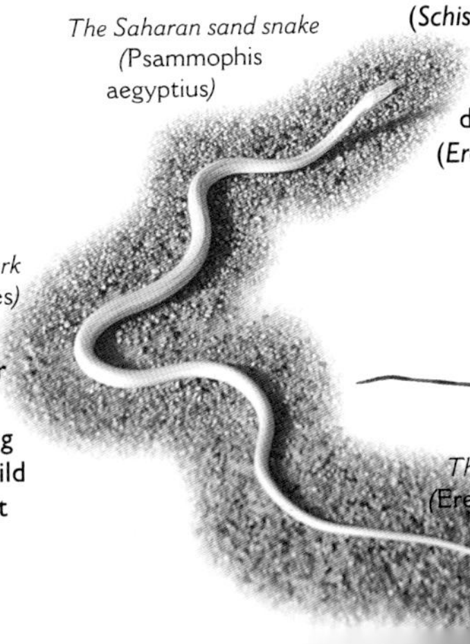

The Saharan sand snake
(Psammophis aegyptius)

An agama
(Pseudotrapelus sinaitus)

Sandfish
(Scincus scincus)

The painted lady
(Vanessa cardui)

frequently, especially after it has rained, in the valleys of Gilf Kebir and Gebel Uweinat, and is often associated with the spiny zilla (*Zilla spinosa*).

The desert locust
(Schistocerca gregaria)

Other invertebrates in the park are the desert locust (*Schistocerca gregaria*), the lesser emperor (*Anax parthenope*) and the desert pebble mantis (*Eremiaphila zetterstedti*).

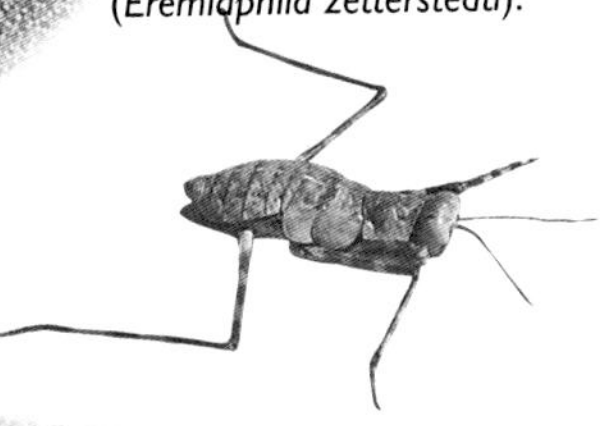

The desert pebble mantis
(Eremiaphila zetterstedti)

The Flora

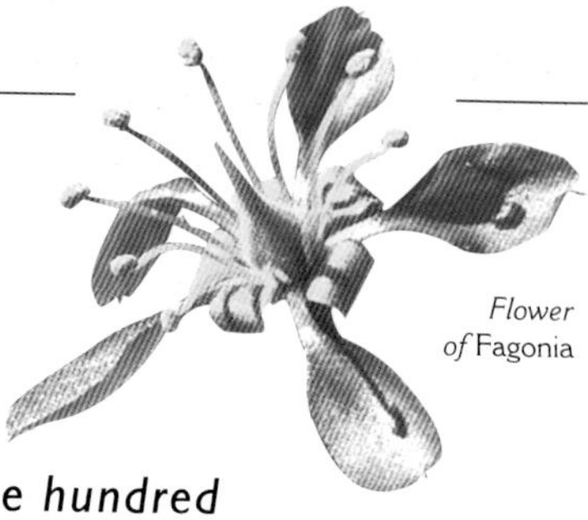

Flower of Fagonia

Incredible as it may seem, there are about one hundred plant species in the GKNP that have adapted to this extremely arid climate. Most of them live on the beds of the large wadis.

Gilf Kebir. Wadi Hamra after the rains in March 2009
Acacia tortilis raddiana, A. ehrenbergiana, Maerua crassifolia *and* Zilla spinosa

The Gilf Kebir and Gebel Uweinat massifs rise abruptly from the vast and often seemingly sterile plains of southwest Egypt. However, areas that support life emerge here in the mountains among the variety of geomorphologic structures, whose particular ecological features produce a number of species and an abundance of vegetation that are astonishing for such an extreme desert environment.

Probably the most striking element of plant life in the ***Gilf Kebir*** are the acacia populations in the wide valleys of the Abu Ras Plateau, which here and there look like an open savanna landscape.

These valleys lie some 100–200 meters below

Acacia tortilis raddiana

Zilla spinosa

the plateau surface and are filled with alluvial fine sediments, so that the rare rainwater that flows from the plateaus is stored and protected against evaporation.

The sparsely populated forests, consisting of *Acacia tortilis raddiana*, *A. ehrenbergiana*, *Maerua crassifolia* and *Balanites aegyptiaca*, and the rich undergrowth appearing here and there among grasses and dwarf-shrubs (including, among others, *Panicum turgidum*, *Centropodia forskalii*, *Stipagrostis rigidifolia*, *Zilla spinosa*, *Fagonia indica* and *Pulicaria undulata*) echo the 'Sahara savannas' leading to the Sahel belt, and are at the same time relics of a type of vegetation that millenniums ago was prevalent throughout the entire Sahara.

However, the wind-exposed plateaus, which are cold in winter, are difficult habitats for plants and therefore sustain a very scanty vegetation cover. The flora shows more of a resemblance to the deserts in the north of Egypt.

The vegetation is concentrated first of all on the basalt hills and the

Aerva javanica

small drainage courses with, for example, *Anastatica hierochuntica* or the Jericho rose, *Salsola imbricata* and *Blepharis edulis*.

Ranged along the narrow valleys of the south plateau, like strings of pearls, are small hillocks of *Fagonia arabica* and *Stipagrostis acutiflora*, which usually lie along gravel terraces.

However, every 10 to 20 years, after exceptional rainfall, the sandy fans leading to the foothills of the escarpment are also studded with quantities of grasses and herbs (e.g. *Monsonia nivea*, *Eremobium aegyptiacum* and *Citrullus colocynthis*), a plant community related to the camel pastures (*gizzu*) of the Wadi Howar in Sudan.

The flora and vegetation of ***Gebel Uweinat*** are characterized by the isolated location of this mountain in the midst of the extremely arid Eastern Sahara.

For many millennia, during which the climate changed to a great degree, the massif was the only location in the region offering refuge to

Anastatica hierochuntica

plants and animals in extremely dry periods, and at the beginning of more humid periods pathways for re-population were formed. Indeed, the towering mountains almost

Shrub of Fagonia

Citrullus colocynthis

2,000 meters high contain permanent watering places, and the vegetation is clearly divided into zones, from the warm-arid foot of the mountain to the cooler but stony summit area.

Furthermore, it is here, in the border zone between summer and winter rain regimes, that two floristic kingdoms converge (Holarctic and Palaeotropic).

Indeed, in this part of the Sahara the mountains are a 'hot spot' of biodiversity, and the number of species per unit area is three times higher than in the nearest massif, the Ennedi in Chad.

The 87 botanical species documented so far belong to 37 plant families, the majority being herbage (Poaceae), pulses (Leguminosae) and the typical Saharan Zygophyllaceae.

The vegetation can be classified according to geological subsoil, altitude belt and availability of water.

In the deep levels of the sandstone mountains

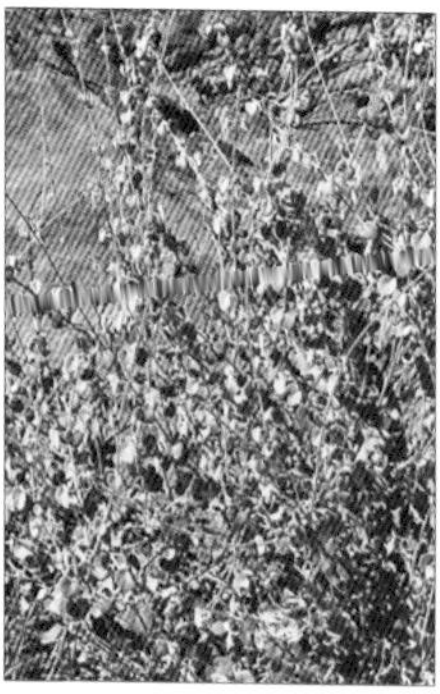

Pergularia tomentosa

(e.g. in Karkur Talh) Acacia-Panicum savannas can be found, with *Acacia tortilis raddiana*, *A. ehrenbergiana*, and *Maerua crassifolia*, as well as an often blooming undergrowth of *Pergularia tomentosa*, *Aerva javanica*, *Morettia philaeana* and *Crotalaria thebaica*, while in the high levels *Lavandula antineae* and *Ochradenus baccatus* dominate.

The most important types of plants on gneiss and granite are *Cleome droserifolia* and *Fagonia thebaica* in the wadis, and *Salvadora persica* as well as *Ficus cordata* in the gorges.

Reeds (*Phragmites australis*, *Typha domingensis* and *Juncus rigidus*) mark permanent watering places and gueltas, which form luxuriant green areas in this blazing rocky desert.

While on the whole the vegetation of Gebel Uweinat is determined by flora originating in tropical Africa, particularly the mountainous regions of East Africa, the influence

Morettia philaeana

of Saharan floristic elements clearly dominates towards the summit regions.

In contrast to other central Saharan mountains, because of the lower summits and the extreme climate, no vegetation types of a Mediterranean character can be found here.

Gebel Uweinat: Panicum turgidum *and* Acacia tortilis

The Climate

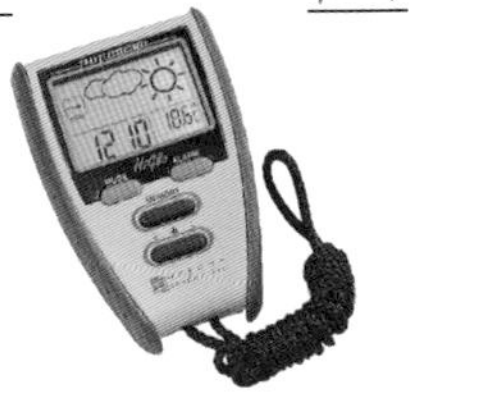

The almost total absence of rainfall, the high maximum temperature, and the great difference in temperature between day and night, all make this a very inhospitable region. But this is not always the case: in fact, many months are suitable for visits to this region.

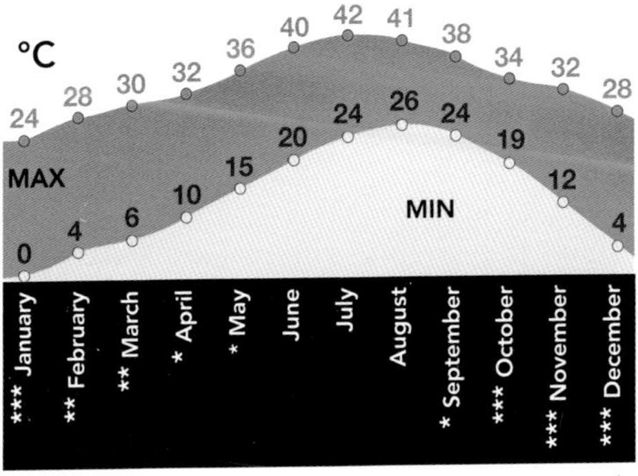

Minimun and maximum temperatures with the best months to visit the area (=medium; **=good;***=perfect)*

The typical climate of the Gilf Kebir and the Great Sand Sea regions is extremely arid, with less than five millimeters of **rainfall** per year and with very high maximum and incredibly low minimum temperatures. As far as the rainfall is concerned, the exception to the rule is the Gebel Uweinat area which, thanks to the altitude of the massif, attracts the humid monsoonal winds that produce an average annual rainfall of 10 millimeters, enough to result in moderate plant growth.

Signs of the arrival of the khamsin *wind*

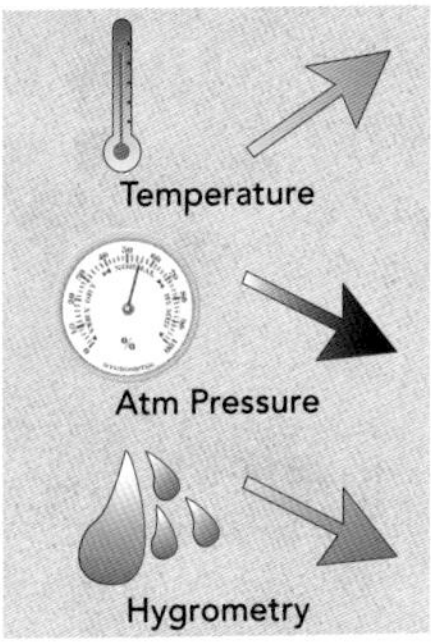

And as for the **temperature**, whoever has traveled in these regions can attest to the truth of the old Berber proverb, "The desert is a cold place where the sun is hot." The difference between the maximum and minimum temperature, and above all the speed of this change, are so extreme that they give rise to the disintegration of the rocks (thermoclastis or insolation weathering).

While it is true that the high maximum temperatures make this region almost inaccessible in the summer, that is, from June to August, in autumn and spring the temperature is quite favorable.

However, from mid-February to the end of April visitors should be careful, because this is the period when there may be a strong southerly wind, called *khamsin* or '50-day wind' in Arabic, which causes strong and bothersome sandstorms.

The rapid and marked variations in temperature cause rocks to crack

The Gilf Kebir Plateau

In this region, which is arid and inhospitable, there are impressive morphological analogies with the planet Mars. Here the water and wind have left their indelible traces, and prehistoric populations have bequeathed an extraordinary artistic heritage.

The wadis of Gilf Kebir viewed from the Abu Ras Plateau

The Gilf Kebir or 'Great Barrier', as it was named in 1926 by the man who discovered it, Prince Kamal el-Din Hussein, is an imposing rocky mass with a total area of 15,700 square kilometers.

Situated at the southern tip of the Great Sand Sea, Gilf Kebir is a plateau that lies 300 meters over the surrounding desert, which has an average altitude of 700 m.

The Gilf Kebir Plateau is divided into two areas that are quite different morphologically: the *Abu Ras Plateau* to the north and the *Kamal el-Din Plateau* to the southeast, separated by a strip of the Great Sand Sea that runs between the two plateaus and that the topographer Patrick Clayton explored in 1931, calling it 'the gap'.

This gap, which is linked to the presence of a fault with a NNW-SSE orientation, corresponds on the terrain to a broad trough known as the *Wadi Assib* (Arduous Valley). On a level with the gap, a pass discovered in 1933 by the Hungarian explorer László Almásy, who named it *al-Aqaba* (the Hill), allows one to go from the eastern to the western side of the Gilf and vice versa.

The Kamal el-Din Plateau has a total area of 7,500 square kilometers (almost the size of the island of Corsica), extends for 125 kilometers latitude, has a maximum width of 80 km, and is as much as 1,091 meters above sea level.

The two plateaus are traversed by many wadis, some of which are dozens of kilometers long, the obvious remains of a complex network of ancient rivers that flowed here at the end of the

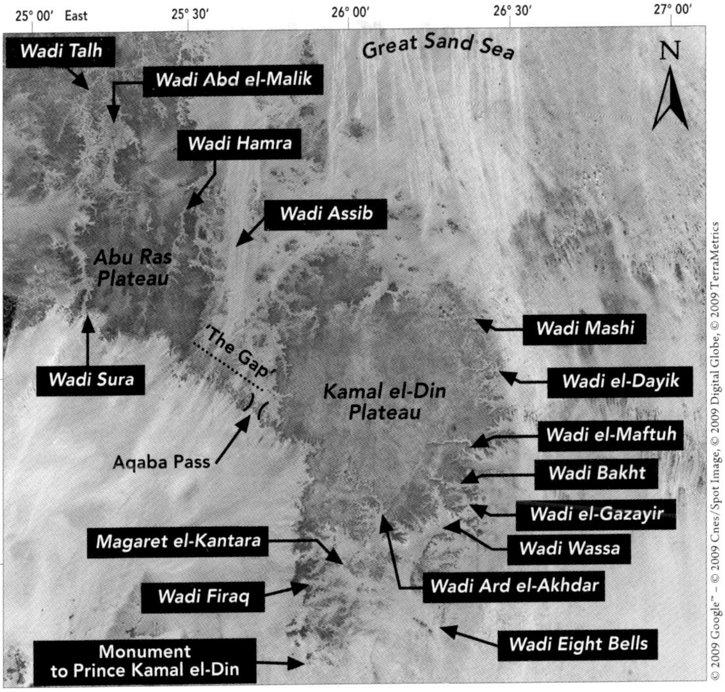

A satellite view of the Gilf Kebir

Tertiary period and during the Quaternary.

The Abu Ras Plateau is dissected by the huge ***Wadi Abd el-Malik*** and the ***Wadi Hamra*** (Red Valley), which run in a rectilinear North-South course, and by the smaller *Wadi Talh* (Acacia Valley), which is to be considered a tributary of the Wadi Abd el-Malik.

Opening eastward on the Kamal el-Din Plateau are the *Wadi Mashi* (Walking Valley), the *Wadi el-Dayik* (Narrow Valley), the *Wadi el-Maftuh* (Open Valley), the ***Wadi Bakht*** (Valley of Luck), the *Wadi el-Gazayir* (Isolated Valley), the *Wadi Wassa* (Wide Valley), the *Wadi Ard el-Akhdar* (Valley of the Green Earth), which is really an immense lateral branch of the Wadi Wassa, the *Wadi Firaq* (Valley of Separation), and the *Eight Bells Wadi*. Both the Wadi Wassa and the Wadi Firaq have easily negotiable tracks that allow one to pass from one side of the Gilf Kebir to the other. However, you must be very cautious in the Wadi Wassa, which still has land mines dating to the Second World War.

The southern end of the Gilf is marked by a cairn with a tablet, known as the **Monument to Prince Kamal el-Din**.

On the western side of the Gilf Kebir is the area of the ***Wadi Sura*** (Picture Valley), which has around twenty sites with examples of prehistoric rock art, the most famous of which are the **Cave of the Swimmers** and the **Foggini-Mestikawi Cave**, which was discovered in 2002.

The Wadi Assib and its complex network of dunes

The Exploration of the Gilf Kebir

The exploration of the Gilf Kebir was carried out by a handful of men of different nationalities who dedicated their lives to this region, following the footsteps of the person who discovered it in 1926, Prince Kamal el-Din Hussein.

The first explorers of Gilf Kebir: Prince Kamal el-Din with László Almásy, wing commander Penderel, Sir Robert Clayton-East-Clayton, and Ralph Bagnold in a photo taken in the 1930s

The only son of Sultan Hussein Kamil (1853–1917), Prince Kamal el-Din was due to succeed him on the throne of Egypt, but out of his great love of the desert and in order to devote all his energy to exploring it, he renounced his dynastic rights in favor of his uncle Ahmed Fuad.

From 1923 to 1926 he made several expeditions into the Western Desert with Ford motor vehicles and Citroën half-tracks.

The prince went as far south as Gebel Uweinat, which had just been discovered by Hassanein Bey, and in early 1926 he discovered a grand plateau that emerged from the sand; he named it Gilf Kebir, the 'Great Barrier'. That same year marked the beginning of

One of the half-tracks built by the Citroën firm for Prince Kamal el-Din's expeditions

HRH Prince Kamal el-Din Hussein (1874–1932)

László Almásy (1895–1951)

the adventures in the Egyptian desert of the Hungarian explorer László Almásy, a complex and controversial person who is now well known as the protagonist of the film *The English Patient* and who carried out many expeditions in the desert, some with the financial aid of Prince Kamal el-Din.

In 1930 the Gilf Kebir region also began to be explored by Major Ralph Alger Bagnold, an extraordinary figure who was not only a British army officer, but also an explorer, topographer and expert of the physics of sand dunes. In 1940 he founded a special desert patrol corps, the famous Long Range Desert Group. In March 1932 Almásy went to Gilf Kebir together with the topographer Patrick Clayton—who for two years had spent all his time painstakingly mapping the region lying between the Nile and Gebel Uweinat—Sir Robert Clayton-East-Clayton and the pilot Hubert Wilson Godfrey Jones Penderel (1890–1943). The expedition also had a small *De Havilland Gypsy Moth* airplane at its disposal. During a survey flight over the north-eastern side of the Gilf they spotted an unknown luxuriant valley that in Almásy's opinion could correspond to the mythical lost oasis of Zerzura. The same year Patrick Clayton made the first East-West crossing of the Great Sand Sea, where he discovered some fragments of mysterious glass that he named *Libyan Desert Silica Glass*.

The following years, from 1933 to 1938, Almásy, Bagnold and Patrick Clayton, together with the archaeologist and explorer William Boyd Kennedy Shaw (1901–79), carried out a series of new expeditions, during which they discovered and documented new aspects of the Gilf Kebir region.

Then in 1940, after the outbreak of the Second World War, the heroic period of the first explorers of the Gilf came to an end and the region, together with the entire Western Desert, became a strategic military theater that witnessed endeavors that had nothing more to do with geographic discoveries. Bagnold and Clayton joined up with the Long Range Desert Group, while Almásy donned a German officer's uniform.

When the war ended the Gilf Kebir and Western Desert were forgotten for quite some time, and it was only in the 1960s that the tracks were once again used, this time by members of scientific missions, including one organized by NASA in 1978 to study the morphological analogies this region had with the planet Mars.

In the 1970s Samir Lama, an eclectic figure and a polyglot, founded a travel agency in the desert, thus opening up this amazing region to tourism and marking the beginning of a new era.

Patrick Clayton (1896–1962)

Ralph Alger Bagnold (1896–1990)

Samir Lama (1931–2004)

The Prehistory

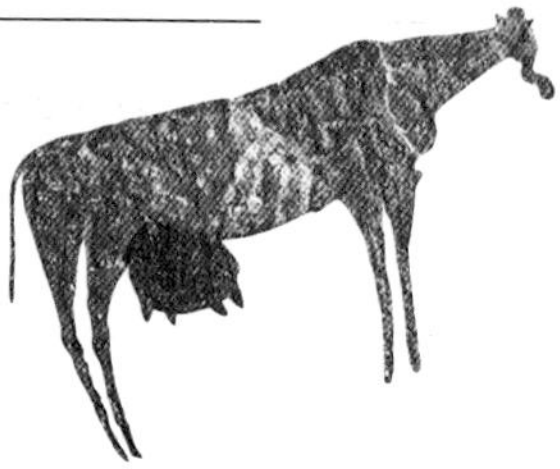

Studies carried out in the Gilf Kebir area have revealed the existence of a Neolithic pastoral society rich in artistic expression the development of which was determined by major changes in the climate.

Rock paintings in the famous Cave of the Swimmers in the Wadi Sura (Gilf Kebir)

In correspondence with the apex of the last glacial period (the so-called LGM or Last Glacial Maximum) about 21,000 years ago, the Sahara had an area almost double that of the present-day desert, and its physical features were similar, with an extremely arid climate. Then, about 11,700 years ago, at the beginning of the Holocene epoch, the climate changed drastically, becoming more humid and rainy, thus transforming vast expanses of sand into savannas with lakes and rivers. This humid phase, the result of the northward shifting of the monsoonal belt, corresponded to the settlement in the entire Gilf Kebir National Park area of numerous populations. At first these were hunters and gatherers who, at a later stage, between 7000 and

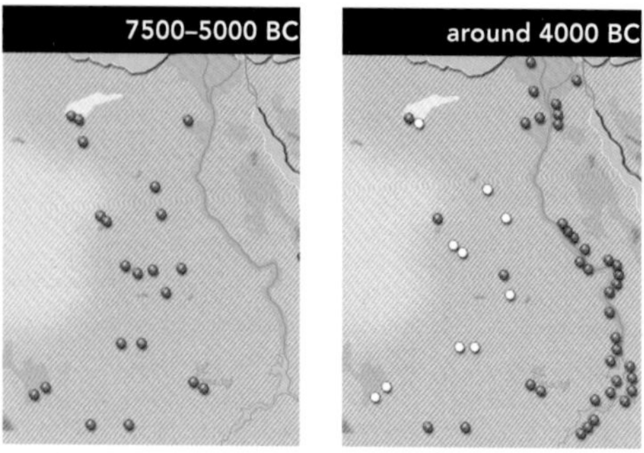

The archaeological sites in the Western Desert in 7500–5000 BC and then around 4000 BC: the ancient populations moved eastwards because of a drier and drier climate (from Kuper & Kröpelin, 2006; modified)

The mysterious circle discovered by Bagnold in the northern Gilf area is probably one of the first astronomical calendars in human history

5300 BC, gave rise to pastoral communities based on the domesticated livestock. This period has bequeathed us an extraordinary artistic heritage represented by rock paintings and carvings that document the existence of a highly developed social system and a magic and religious praxis that could have probably been the source of certain myths of ancient Egypt itself.

A mysterious circle made up of upright stones, which Ralph Bagnold discovered in the northern part of the Gilf in 1930, leads one to presume that the prehistoric populations in the region had already acquired a certain level of scientific knowledge. In fact, the circle has a precise astronomical alignment and most probably also served as a sort of calendar connected to the existence of a ceremonial area. A similar structure was found at *Nabta Playa*, about 100 kilometers west of Abu Simbel.

Around 5,300 BC the monsoonal belt returned southward, creating, in the Gilf Kebir and the entire eastern Sahara area, a new change in the climate, which became drier and drier, forcing the local populations to move southward and eastward in search of sources of water, even as far as the Nile Valley. Thus began a new chapter in the history of this region.

A prehistoric mortar with its pestle, found in the Gilf Kebir region

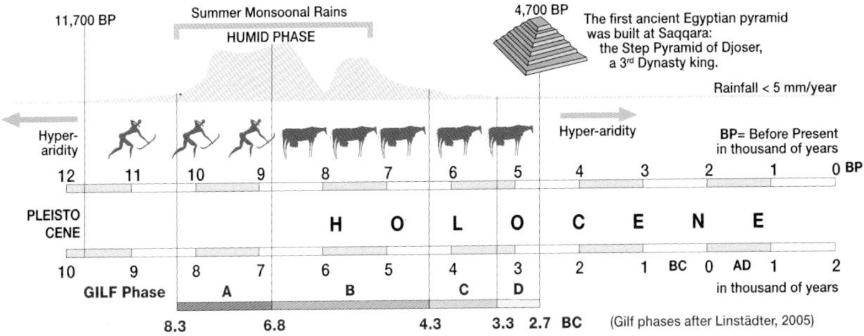

The climatic changes in the Gilf Kebir region in the last 12,000 years

Wadi Abd el-Malik

This wadi is the largest and, in certain respects, the most mysterious in the entire Gilf Kebir. It abounds in prehistoric sites and still bears traces of its original vegetation.

Ibrahim Abd el-Malik, after whom the valley was named

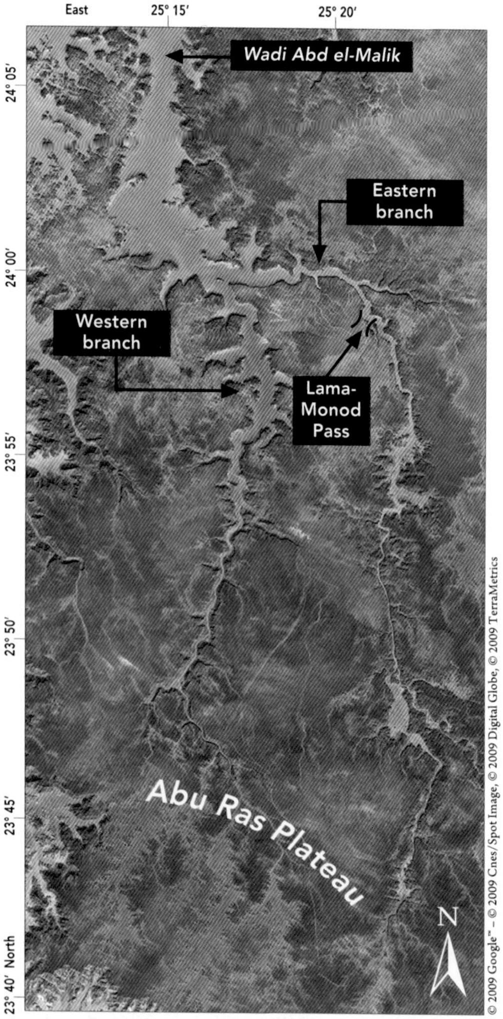

This satellite photograph clearly shows the southern portion of Wadi Abd el-Malik, which splits into two distinct branches

The Wadi Abd el-Malik, which runs through the Abu Ras Plateau along a north-south alignment for about 120 kilometers, was first explored by Almásy and Penderel, who arrived there in May 1933 by following the indications given them by a Bedouin cameleer from Kufra (Libya), Ibrahim Abd el-Malik el-Zueia. The two explorers, who had already flown over the zone in a small *De Havilland Gypsy Moth* plane in April 1932, discovering two wadis with vegetation, now found numerous acacia trees and the remains of a Tebu camp.

Almásy and Penderel also explored another wadi situated in a more westerly position, again with vegetation: the *Wadi Talh* or Acacia Valley.

That same year, Patrick Clayton, accompanied by Lady Dorothy, the widow of Sir Robert Clayton-East-Clayton, succeeded in entering a third valley in the same area, the *Wadi Hamra*, which also

The Gypsy Moth

The rock paintings representing cattle discovered by Bagnold

Lama-Monod Pass.

The rock walls of the central part of this branch contain numerous petroglyphs representing wild animals, including giraffes, and livestock. It was here that Ralph Alger Bagnold, during his spring 1938 expedition, found a shelter with paintings depicting bovids, the sole example known in the northern section of the Gilf.

had vegetation. Had they possibly found the fascinating and mysterious Zerzura oasis with its three valleys? However, as far as we know today, the Wadi Abd el-Malik has no waterhole or spring source, but Ibrahim, who grazed his camels there, assured the explorers that there was water in the eastern branch.

The Wadi Abd el-Malik is rather wide to the north and splits into a western and eastern branch; access to the latter can be had also by descending from the Abu Ras Plateau through the

THE LEGEND OF ZERZURA

In 1835 the famous Egyptologist John G. Wilkinson related that an Arab had spoken to him about a mysterious and unknown oasis called Zerzura, *which is described in a famous medieval manuscript called* The Book of Hidden Pearls, *which is nothing more or less than a guidebook for treasure hunters. In this description the mysterious oasis comprised three green valleys and was rich in springs, palm trees, and animals, including many birds. Many twentieth-century explorers attempted in vain to find Zerzura, a place name that, curiously enough, coincides with the Arabic name for a bird that is widespread in the Western Desert—the white-crowned wheatear (*Oenanthe leucopyga*). Almásy was convinced he had found the mythical oasis in the area that corresponds to the Abd el-Malik, Talh and Hamra wadis, but the truth is, Zerzura is still a mystery.*

View of one of the lateral branches of the Wadi Abd el-Malik

Wadi Hamra

Many people consider this valley, whose main features are its stunning red sand and the great number of acacias, the most beautiful in the entire Gilf Kebir region. However, the presence of vegetation and wild animals means that access to this wadi is necessarily limited.

Wadi Hamra viewed from the top of the Abu Ras Plateau

Whoever arrives at the Wadi Hamra, a place name that in Arabic means 'Red Valley', cannot help being astounded by its beauty and the bright red color of its sand, so rich in ferrous oxide, which imparts this particular hue. Here there are many large umbrella thorns (*Acacia raddiana*) arranged in lines, especially along the eastern side of the wadi.

The Wadi Hamra, which dissects the mass of the Abu Ras Plateau for about twenty kilometers in a north-south direction, was first explored in 1933 by

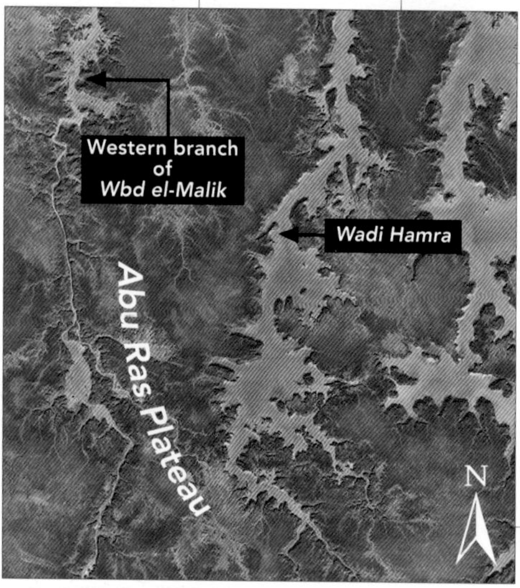

A satellite view of Wadi Hamra

*Many petroglyphs in the wadi represent wild animals, most of which are giraffes (*Giraffa camelopardatis*)*

Patrick Clayton and was visited two years later by the German scientists Leo Frobenius and Hans Rhotert, who discovered the first rock carvings there. In fact, this wadi boasts a great many artistic sites with rock carvings, which are divided into three groups located in the central part and near the head of the valley, while Hamra has no rock paintings at all. The main subjects of the petroglyphs in the Wadi Hamra, which many scholars feel are the most ancient ones in the entire region, are wild animals, including numerous giraffes, gazelles and oryxes, cattle, and some illustrations of dogs.

A petroglyph of a canid

Although there are no longer any springs or other sources of water in the valley, during the period when it was first explored the Wadi Hamra was particularly verdant and suitable for grazing camels.

To this day, besides the acacia trees, there are many bushes in the valley. The most representative are *Fagonia thebaica*, *Zilla spinosa* and *Maerua crassifolia*, which are food for the various wild animals (gazelles and Barbary sheep). Furthermore, a real surprise is in store for those who see the wadi after heavy rainfall, when it takes on its original appearance and looks like a savanna (see photo on page 10).

Petroglyphs representing canids, cattle and wild animals

Wadi Bakht

A stone tool

For thousands of years this majestic wadi was the home of Neolithic hunters and herders and has been the object of long-term studies that have shed new light on the prehistory of the Gilf region.

View of the Wadi Bakht downhill from the barrier dune. This site is extremely fragile and access there is regulated: it is forbidden to walk on the dune and the paleolake

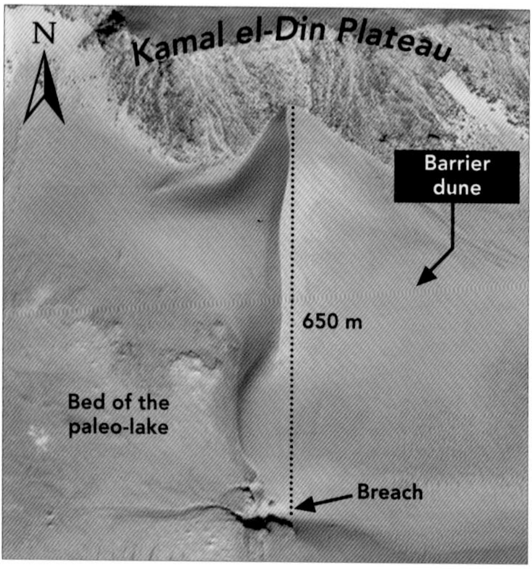

Satellite view of the last section of the Wadi Bakht

The Wadi Bakht, which in Arabic means 'valley of luck', opens onto the eastern side of the Gilf Kebir, between the Wadi Maftuh to the north and the Wadi el-Gazayir to the south. The Wadi Bakht cuts through the Gilf for 22 km and its distinctive feature is a large dune thirty meters high that blocks it crosswise at a distance of 19 km from the access. At the top of this barrier, which was breached around 3500 BC, there was once an ancient lake (10,000 years ago) that had a maximum depth of nine meters and

The breach that allowed water to flow through the wadi

The large dune that blocks the Wadi Bakht

a capacity of 100,000 cubic meters of water. Stratigraphic analyses of the lacustrine deposits (known as *playa* deposits) more than 8 m thick have provided extremely important data regarding the paleoenvironment. In this valley, which was particularly favorable for human settlements, there is documentation of prehistoric populations that lived here from 8300 to 3500 BC. At first their economy was based on hunting and gathering, while it became pastoral in the latter phase of the Neolithic period.

The inhabitants of this region employed different strategies in the use of the land, based on the prevailing climatic and geomorphological conditions. Thus, initially, during the so-called Gilf B phase (6800–4300 BC), the many prehistoric settlements in the wadi were distributed near the huge dune barrier, moving also to the surrounding plateau in the following Gilf C phase (4300– 3300 BC).

The study of the Wadi Bakht had begun already in 1938 with Olivier Myers, the archaeologist of the Bagnold-Mond expedition, and was continued in a twenty-year research campaign carried out by the University of Cologne as part of the B.O.S. (*Besiedlungsgeschichte der Ost-Sahara*) and ACACIA (Arid Climate Adaptation and Cultural Innovation in Africa) projects, which made a fundamental contribution to our knowledge of the region's climate in the last 12,000 years.

The deposits corresponding to the bed of the ancient lake

Eight Bells

During the Second World War, the English laid out an airport in this broad valley bounded by a series of eight bell-shaped hills. Its remains are still in good condition.

The eight bell-shaped hills, characteristic of the Eight Bells site, viewed from a satellite

At the southern border of the Gilf Kebir, south of the Wassa and Firaq wadis, there is a series of eight bell-shaped hills of Paleozoic sandstone that were pushed upward by endogenic forces: the entire area, which has been named 'Eight Bells', is a vast, open wadi that drains southward.

In the plain opposite the hills are the virtually intact remains of an airport used by the British in the Second World War.

A large arrow that indicated the direction the planes should land in, and the name of the site, made up of hundreds of empty fuel tanks, can still be clearly seen.

The name of the site

The arrow used to indicate the direction of the plane landings

Magaret el-Kantara

Also known as Shaw's Cave, this shelter is decorated with extremely beautiful paintings, mostly of cattle, a testament to the high artistic level achieved by the Neolithic pastoral culture of the Gilf Kebir region.

A group of cattle painted with red and white pigment on the wall of the shelter

In January 1935 the archaeologist William Kennedy Shaw together with Rupert Harding Newman discovered this shelter, which opens eastward at a height of about 100 meters on the promontory separating the Wadi Wassa and Wadi Firaq, in the southern section of the Gilf Kebir, roughly 40 kilometers south of Wadi Bakht. The shelter, which is 4 m high and 15 m long, is of the utmost importance both because of the quality of its paintings, which depict cattle for the most part, and because it is the sole example of rock paintings in the southeastern section of the Gilf.

Newman came to the conclusion that some of these paintings were executed about 8,000 years ago.

The entrance to Magaret el-Kantara

View from the interior of the shelter

Wadi Sura

This is the most famous site in the Gilf Kebir, with the Cave of the Swimmers, some of the paintings of which, now quite deteriorated, document a paleoenvironment very different from the present-day one, its distinctive feature being the presence of water.

The Cave of the Swimmers and the nearby Cave of the Archers at the Wadi Sura

Wadi Sura or Picture Valley opens onto the northwestern side of the Gilf Kebir and cuts through the mountain for a few hundred meters.

It was here that László Almásy discovered, in October 1933, during the expedition made with the ethnographer Leo Frobenius and the archaeologist Hans Rhotert, the famous **Cave of the Swimmers**, which was immortalized in the film *The English Patient* (1996). Obviously there is no correspondence (except for the reproduction of the drawings) between what one sees in the movie and the real cave, just as there is no relation between the fictional Almásy in the film version played by Ralph Fiennes and the true Hungarian explorer.

László Almásy in front of the Cave of the Swimmers

However, there is no doubt that despite their poor state of preservation, the paintings in this cave (which is really an open

These enigmatic figures painted on the walls of the Cave of the Swimmers seem to be swimming. At present, the paintings are in an alarmingly deteriorated state, and if no restoration work is done their very survival is in jeopardy

shelter a few meters deep) truly captivate visitors, making them imagine what this region—one of the most arid in the world—must have been like 10,000 years ago, at the time when the so-called 'green Sahara' abounded in water and small lakes.

Some of the persons in these works are depicted in a horizontal position with their arms stretched in front of them, as if they were swimming or even diving, hence the name given to the cave by Almásy. Besides the 'swimmers', whose real meaning is still an enigma, there are other human figures divided into various groups.

Human figures with the triangular bust typical of the 'Sura style', with 'swimmers' below

Tall, elongated human figures in the Cave of the Archers

The walls with the paintings consist of a layer of extremely friable sandstone that tends to peel off the rock underneath, which has led to the loss of many paintings and the creation

Satellite view of the Wadi Sura area

of wide gaps in the works.

Next to the Cave of the Swimmers is another shelter, which is smaller and is decorated with large human figures, men armed with bows and arrows (hence the name, **Cave of the Archers**), and animals, which have been almost entirely obliterated.

In 2002 the fame of the Wadi Sura increased enormously thanks to the chance discovery of a new shelter decorated with hundreds of paintings, this time, fortunately, in a perfect state of preservation, which make it the most beautiful and interesting rock art site in the Gilf Kebir region. It is located about eleven kilometers northwest of the Cave of the Swimmers and was immediately named the 'Sistine Chapel of Prehistory'. It is about sixty meters above the plateau, which corresponds to an ancient lake whose remains are still easy to see.

The persons who made this amazing discovery were the Italian Massimo and Jacopo Foggini, who explored the region with a veteran of the Western Desert, Colonel Ahmed Mestikawi, who served as the guide and also saw to the logistic organization of the expedition.

The discovery gave rise to disputes regarding the name to be given the new

The entrance of the Foggini-Mestikawi Cave

The Foggini-Mestikawi Cave is decorated with paintings in a perfect state of preservation, the most striking of which are the 300 or so negative hands

A large headless, feline-like monster

Negative hands and representations of human beings

site: Foggini Cave, Mestikawi Cave or simply New Cave, while the Germans preferred Wadi Sura 2 and the French liked Cave of the Beasts... There is still no official name for the cave, so that it is probably convenient to use the most common name, the 'Foggini-Mestikawi Cave'.

The basic iconographic motifs of this site are the innumerable negative impressions of human hands, a theme widespread in European rock art whose meaning is still a mystery.

Other iconographic elements are small human figures, the many representations of wild animals (giraffes), depictions of swimmers executed in a style analogous to that in the cave discovered by Almásy, strange headless beasts, and an enigmatic being that is half-human and half-animal with monstrous features that seems to have some relationship with the swimmers. On the other hand, representations of domestic animals and pastoral scenes are

Representations of human figures, hunters,

11 MAY 2002: THE DISCOVERY

After the umpteenth disappointment caused by the increasingly precarious conditions of the Cave of the Swimmers, indications of earlier travelers help us to spot various small paintings and rock carvings at the foot of the Gilf Kebir cliff, and we skirt it while moving northward. At the base of a steep sandy ascent are the remains of a fossil lake and, further up, what might be a shelter... Temperature 49 °C in the automobile. I tell my son Jacopo to climb up to have a look. Most reluctantly he scrambles up the loose sand and disappears behind the crest. He reappears a few minutes later, shouting 'Thousands! Thousands!' Paying no heed to the heat and climb, in a few minutes we are all up there... That evening, in the camp, we write and sign, together with Ahmed Mestikawi, who is the guide of this expedition, the record of the discovery, in which we declare that, subject to the agreement of the Egyptian authorities, on 11 May 2002 at 4:50 pm we discovered the 'Foggini Cave' in the 'Wadi el-Mestikawi'.

Massimo Foggini

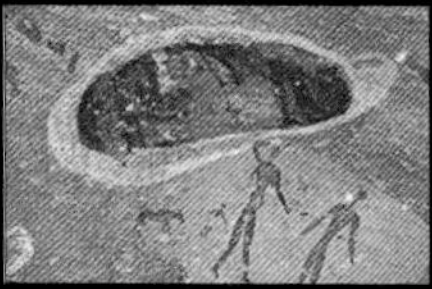

Human figures in front of a dark, oval shape: could it be an ancient lake?

It is difficult to imagine the true meaning of these paintings, but one cannot help wondering whether there is some distant relationship with elements such as the dead who swim or the all-devouring monsters that characterize the iconography of the ancient Egyptian *Book of the Dead* written thousands of years later.

In a short time this site became a major attraction, a must for anyone visiting the Gilf Kebir, and in fact thousands of persons come here every year, with the consequent problems for the conservation of these masterpieces of Saharan rock art.

The scientific study of the site began in 2009, carried out by the Heinrich Barth Institut of Cologne and headed by Rudolph Kuper, one of the best-known specialists of the Gilf Kebir area.

Representation of a large, headless hybrid creature associated with the swimmers

Human figures that seem to be mirrored in a river represented by a crack in the rock

On the Abu Ras Plateau

The top of the Abu Ras Plateau is a vast stretch of rocky and dusty land. By going along its edges one has a spectacular view of the deep wadis that cut through the mass of rock.

The dusty Abu Ras Plateau

The uppermost part of the Gilf Kebir comprises two plateaus, *Abu Ras* to the north, and *Kamal el-Din* to the southeast. However, only the former is of easy access and interesting from a touristic standpoint.

The Abu Ras Plateau dominates the entire Wadi Sura area. On an average it is 900 meters above sea level, extends for 140 kilometers and has a maximum width of only 40 kilometers.

The plateau, made up of Paleozoic ferruginous sandstone (the Abu Ras Formation) that lies directly over the Precambrian basement and is in turn covered by Jurassic-Cretaceous deposits, is dissected to the north by two large valleys, the Wadi Abd el-Malik and Wadi Hamra, into which one can descend via two difficult tracks. On the plateau, an easy and well-marked circular track ensures rapid movement. The southernmost point of this track is distinguished

The rocky surface of the plateau

The Lama Memorial *boasts a stupendous panoramic view*

by the so-called *Lama Memorial* (not to be confused with *Lama Point*, which is situated around 17 kilometers further north), a tablet in memory of Samir Lama, who called the site *Bellevue*, since he used to stop here often to admire the landscape.

The plaque in memory of Samir Lama at Bellevue

From this point, proceeding northward, the track skirts and dominates the entire vast area opposite Wadi Sura and arrives at a sandy area nicknamed 'Jericho', where one can see thousands of so-called roses of Jericho (*Anastatica hierochuntica*), an annual plant that has adapted to desert life. Proceeding even further north, the track enters the area of the Wadi Abd el-Malik, into which one can descend by using the *Lama-Monod Pass*, named in honor of the person who discovered it, Samir Lama, who made many expeditions in the Gilf region with the famous French naturalist Théodore Monod (1902–2000).

The 'Jericho' site, with thousands of small 'roses'

The entrance of Lama-Monod Pass, *which affords access down to the Wadi Abd el-Malik*

Théodore Monod (left) and Samir Lama (right)

From the Gilf to Gebel Uweinat

The area between the Gilf Kebir and Gebel Uweinat, which are about 150 kilometers from one another, is very interesting from a geological and historic standpoint as well as for its scenery.

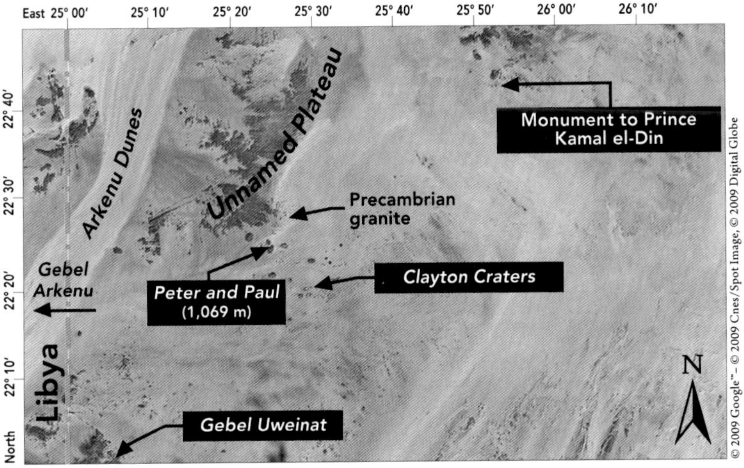

The area between the Gilf Kebir and Gebel Uweinat, bordered to the west by a barrier of dunes

The southern boundary of the Gilf Kebir region is marked by the so-called **Monument to Prince Kamal el-Din**: it was here in 1933 that Almásy placed a tablet with the following dedication written in Arabic: "In memory of HRH Prince Kamal el-Din Hussein, a great explorer

Almásy with the tablet in memory of Prince Kamal el-Din

The monument in memory of Prince Kamal el-Din and Almásy's tablet

of the Libyan desert, [monument] built by persons who appreciate his great achievements." The following year Almásy returned to this site with some members of the Royal Automobile Club of Egypt and constructed, near the monument, the small stone pyramid that still stands there.

The vast plain,

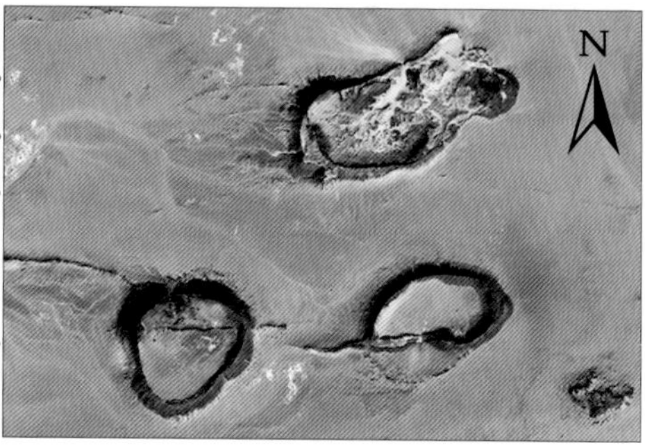

Some of the so-called Clayton Craters *seen from a satellite*

Granite modeled by meteoric agents

consisting for the most part of recent Quaternary deposits, separates Gilf Kebir and Gebel Uweinat and is bounded to the west first by a rocky plateau known as the ***Unnamed Plateau*** and then by a network of dunes called the *Arkenu Dunes*, beyond which, in Libyan territory, is the *Gebel Arkenu*, whose shape looks like a small version of the Gebel Uweinat.

Proceeding southward, cropping up from the Quaternary deposits are very ancient rocks that are part of Paleozoic (Devonian) clastic formations, as well as Precambrian granite and granitoid.

There are also outcrops of much more recent rocks that form Tertiary (Oligocene) and Quaternary basalt and dolerite dikes.

The track passes in the vicinity of a pair of trachyte peaks, the ***Peter and Paul*** mountains (1,069 m), before penetrating the area of the so-called ***Clayton Craters***, discovered in 1932 by Almásy and Sir Robert Clayton. However, it must be said that these impressive formations (the largest of which are 1.5 kilometers in diameter and 100–120 meters high) are not true volcanic craters but rather round dikes formed by magma that seeped through the ancient Paleozoic sandstone and that can still be seen on the edges of the formations.

Lastly, a short distance from the Gebel Uweinat there are extraordinary granitic outcrops that have been eroded and shaped by meteoric agents.

The interior of the largest of the Clayton Craters

Gebel Uweinat

Gebel Uweinat is an isolated mountain (or inselberg) that rises up almost 2,000 m over the desert where the borders of Egypt, Sudan and Libya converge. It played a decisive role in the development of Neolithic societies 10,000 years ago.

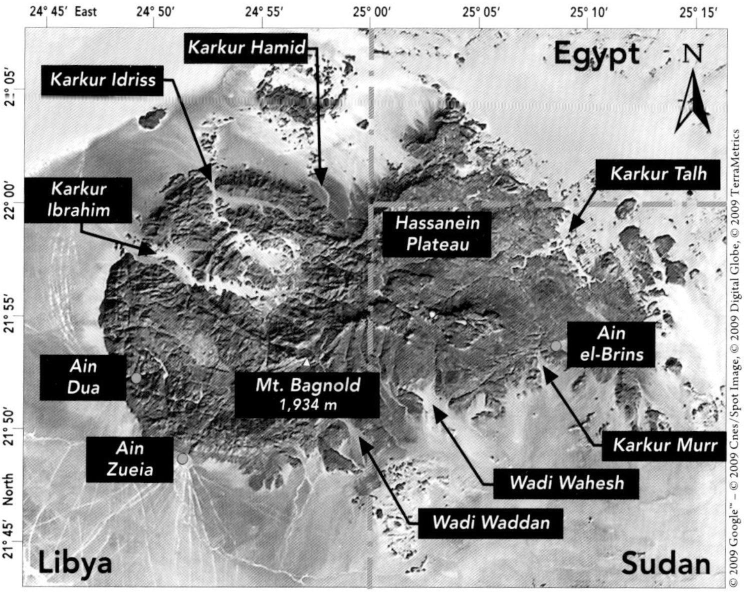

View of Gebel Uweinat from a satellite

Gebel Uweinat, or 'Mountain of Small Springs', is a ring complex with a diameter of around twenty-five kilometers—the residue of a gigantic granitic pluton dating from the Precambrian eon that outcropped about fifty million years ago—which extends eastward in the vast *Hassanein Plateau*.

This granitic complex is dissected by two deep, almost parallel valleys called *Karkur Idriss* and *Karkur Ibrahim*, as well as by a third, smaller valley known as *Karkur Hamid*.

The Hassanein Plateau, made up of Paleozoic sandstone, culminates with Mt. Bagnold, which is 1,934 meters above sea level and is cut through by a vast wadi called *Karkur Talh* or 'Acacia Valley' (*karkur* is a synonym of wadi, while *talh* means acacias) that extends southward with a small valley known as *Karkur Murr*.

Due to its impressive height, Gebel Uweinat attracts clouds of monsoonal origin and thus enjoys occasional rainfall (about ten millimeters per year) that creates the conditions for the growth of flora that is absolutely exceptional in such a hyperarid environment.

Gebel Uweinat has two springs, *Ain Dua* and *Ain Zueia*, and also a well called *Ain el-Brins* (or *Bir Murr*).

The Exploration of Gebel Uweinat

The history of the exploration of Gebel Uweinat is quite different from that of the Gilf region, and the principal figures involved were Ahmed Hassanein Bey, who discovered it in 1923, and the Italians who first made a scientific study of the mountain.

Ahmed Ahmed Hassanein Bey was an adventurous and romantic Egyptian gentleman who was born in Cairo in 1889 and educated at Oxford. In early 1923 he crossed the entire Western Desert with a caravan of camels, starting off from the Mediterranean coast and heading southward for 2,200 miles.

During this journey Hassanein Bey discovered an isolated massif that he named *Gebel Uweinat* or 'Mountain of Small Springs'. The explorer published the results of his expedition in a book with the emblematic title *The Lost Oasis*, and in two long articles that appeared in the September 1924 issue of *National Geographic Magazine* and in the vol. 64, 1924 issue of *Geographical Journal*. These works were the first to record the presence of rock art in this region.

Ahmed Hassanein Bey (1889–1946) during the time of the discovery of Gebel Uweinat

In 1926 Prince Kamal el-Din also arrived and explored Gebel Uweinat.

In January 1931, while the Italian Army occupied the Kufra oasis in Libya, Patrick Clayton led an expedition that went as far as the massif. The following year Ralph

The geologist Ardito Desio during the 1931 mission

The zoologist Lodovico di Caporiacco (1900–51)

Bagnold, together with William Kennedy Shaw, visited Gebel Uweinat; he was the first to conquer the peak and also drew an approximate map of the zone. The summer of 1931 marked the beginning of the 'period of Italian exploration'.

The geologist Ardito Desio (1897–2001) made an early study of Gebel Uweinat that was developed more in depth in 1933 by the Geo-topographical Mission headed by Captain Oreste Marchesi, one of whose members was the zoologist Lodovico di Caporiacco, who wrote a journal of the expedition published with the title *Nel cuore del deserto libico* (In the Heart of the Libyan Desert).

Marchesi and Caporiacco climbed up the Uweinat and found the true summit, which was a few meters higher than the altitude reached by Bagnold, and they named it *Cima Italia* (Italy Peak), present-day

The book Ludovico di Caporiacco wrote about the mission to Gebel Uweinat and the Ain Dua paintings

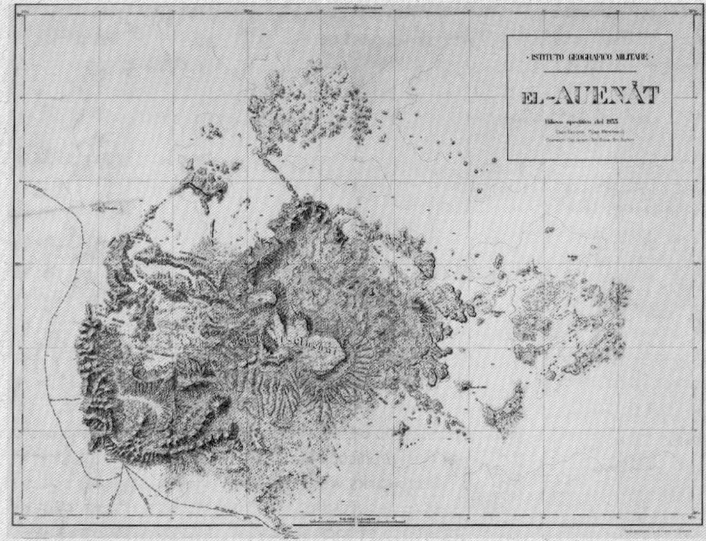

The map of Gebel Uweinat drawn up in 1933 by Oreste Marchesi's expedition and published by the Italian Istituto Geografico Militare *(Military Geographic Institute) of Florence. Its accuracy is simply amazing*

Mt. Bagnold. The Marchesi mission drew up the first detailed topographical map of the region, in a scale of 1:100,000.

In May 1933 the explorer László Almásy reached Gebel Uweinat and met Caporiacco. During his stay there the splendid rock paintings of Ain Dua were discovered, but later on a bitter dispute arose as to who was to be credited with this major achievement.

Professor Montérin (indicated by the arrow) together with Major Rolle and Captain Arkwright in 1934

In October of that same year, Almásy returned to Uweinat, this time with the archaeologist Hans Rhotert and the ethnologist Leo

László Almásy (seated) with Hans Rhotert and Leo Frobenius (at right) in 1933

Frobenius. During their mission they discovered no fewer than 65 new rock art sites in the Karkur Talh area.

Later on, in 1934, the Italian geologist Umberto Montérin (1887–1940), in company with Major Ottavio Rolle, the commander of the Kufra base, climbed up Gebel Uweinat and reached the *Emeri plateau*, discovering, among other things, a cave (rediscovered in 2006 by an Italian expedition) in which there was a spring.

That same year the Royal Air Force (RAF) and the Sudan Defence Force (SDF), commanded by Captain Francis Arkwright, occupied the Karkur Murr area.

Again in 1934 the new Libya-Sudan frontier was established along the 25° E meridian.

In 1937 Ralph Bagnold, together with archaeologists Oliver Myers and Hans Winkler, carried out the interdisciplinary expedition to Gilf Kebir and Gebel Uweinat—under the aegis of the Egypt Exploration Society and with the financial backing of the British archaeologist and chemist Sir Robert Mond—during which the main rock art sites at Karkur Talh were discovered.

During the Second World War and in the immediate post-war period as well the exploratory expeditions at Gebel Uweinat were suspended, and the region became a war zone for the men and materiel of the Long Range Desert Group, which set up camp in the Kufra Oasis after having wrested it from the Italians in March 1941.

Twenty-five years after the end of the war, in 1969, the Desert Rescue Team of the RAF made an expedition to Gebel Uweinat to ascertain the presence of remains of military vehicles or downed airplanes.

In 1968 and 1969 the National Belgian Expedition, an interdisciplinary mission, made the first truly scientific of Gebel Uweinat discovering a series of new and extremely important sites in the Karkur Talh area: to this day a branch of the Karkur Talh is called 'Wadi Belgian'.

The Prehistory

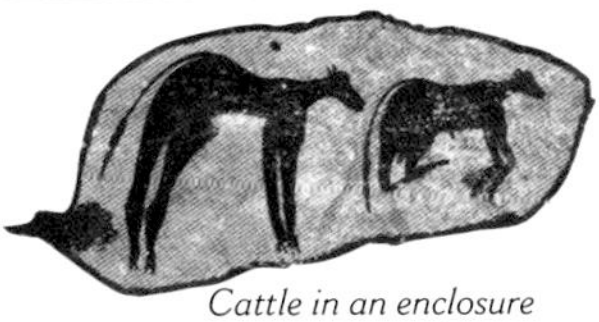

Cattle in an enclosure

The particular geographic and climatic conditions in the Gebel Uweinat favored the development of a pastoral Neolithic community that lived here 12,000–7,000 years ago and produced amazing artistic works that can still be admired.

Karkur Talh painting representing a group of herders, in the 'elongated style', around cattle

Gebel Uweinat is a privileged area where, since 8500 BC, at the beginning of the humid period of the Holocene, many prehistoric people found ideal conditions for the development of a society based at first on hunting and gathering, and then on pastoralism and domesticated livestock.

The life of these populations is documented by hundreds of rock carvings and above all by rock paintings, which make this region one of the most important sites of rock art in the world.

Already noted by Hassanein Bey in 1923, the Uweinat rock art sites were studied by Ludovico di Caporiacco, László Almásy, Hans Rhotert, Leo Frobenius

Two 'elongated style' archers in front of an oryx gazelle

and Hans Winkler from 1933 to 1937, and later on in 1968–69 by the National Belgian Expedition, whose research was conducted for the most part in the Karkur Talh area.

The study of the rock art of the Gebel Uweinat allowed archaeologists to reconstruct the life of these prehistoric groups and their adaptation to an arid or semi-arid environment.

The rock art of Gebel Uweinat reveals the presence of different styles corresponding to the various periods, but the motifs are almost

Painting representing a family of herders with their animals

always the same: wild animals such as giraffes, ostriches and oryxes, and domestic ones like cattle and goats, hunting and pastoral scenes, and representations of everyday family life. On the other hand, such wild animals as elephants and hippopotami are absent.

The most ancient scenes, painted and drawn about 8,000–7,000 years ago, are related to an economy based on hunting and gathering, while the pastoral scenes—which are the most common ones—correspond to an economy based on herding and are datable to 6,000 years ago.

When in 5300 BC the climate of the Sahara began its irreversible change, gradually becoming more and more arid until, around the year 3300 BC, it attained its present configuration, Gebel Uweinat remained an isolated spot, the only source of water within a radius of hundreds of kilometers. The pastoral communities that lived in the neighboring areas such as Gilf Kebir probably moved toward Gebel Uweinat, a region able to guarantee survival for them and their animals. Some groups continued to inhabit the Uweinat area even after 2700 BC, the date that according to scholars marked the definitive abandonment of Gilf Kebir.

Paintings of cattle are the most common ones at Karkur Talh

The rock art of Gebel Uweinat attracts more and more tourists from all over the world

At the time of its discovery in 1923, Gebel Uweinat was not uninhabited as it is now, but was still the home of herders of the Goran and Tebu Negroid populations from the Tibesti region in Chad who grazed their flocks of camels here. They were the last inhabitants of the region.

The aridity of the surrounding desert made Gebel Uweinat an obligatory transit route in the network of the major trans-Saharan roads, a role it continued to play even in modern times, first for the camel caravans that transported goods among Libya, Egypt, Sudan and Chad, and then for the vehicles that eventually brought about the demise of the caravans.

Because of the exceptional importance of the rock art found there, Gebel Uweinat has been proposed as one of the sites to be placed on the UNESCO World Heritage List.

Karkur Talh

This large wadi that extends into the Gebel Uweinat plateau for more than twenty-five kilometers boasts over 4,000 rock art sites, thus making the locality an open-air museum of inestimable value.

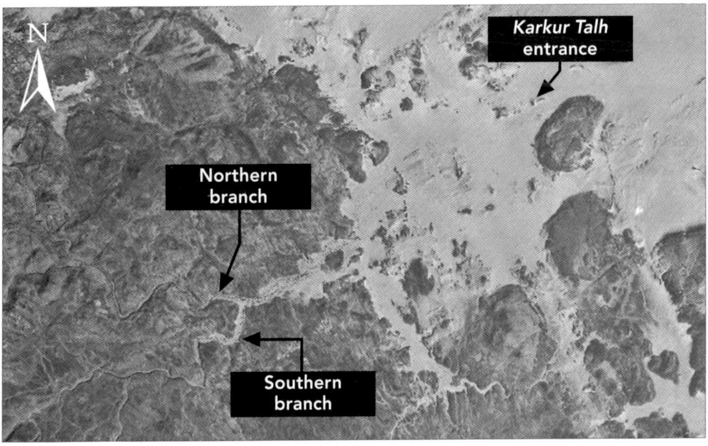

The entrance and northern part of Karkur Talh viewed from a satellite

Karkur Talh means Acacia Valley. In fact, despite the aridity of its initial stretch, which consists of loose sand and dune formations, its central section is the home of the most beautiful forest of acacias (*Acacia tortilis raddiana*) in the entire region as well as of an extremely wide range of shrubs.

But the truly interesting aspect of Karkur Talh, most of which is located in Sudanese territory, consists in the fact that it has a large number of prehistoric sites and some of the most beautiful examples of Saharan rock art, which testify to the settlement here of numerous communities during the Holocene epoch. In the Karkur Talh wadi there are both petroglyphs and wall paintings. The former represent wild animals (especially giraffes), cattle and humans who are almost always associated with the cattle, as well as hunting scenes with

The entrance to Karkur Talh

Acacias (A.tortilis raddiana), a distinctive feature of the central section of Karkur Talh

Barbary sheep, gazelles or other wild animals, which sometimes include depictions of canids.

The camel carvings, on the other hand, date to a recent period.

The paintings were executed with red pigments of different hues, yellows and whites, and they represent only pastoral scenes, which at times are linked to symbolic elements.

Dry mud, a sign of rainfall

The rocky bed of an ancient torrent

A shelter with rock paintings in a branch of the Karkur Talh

The Great Sand Sea

This immense expanse of sand dunes occupying an area of 72,000 square kilometers that lies between the Siwa Oasis and the Gilf Kebir, without a single source of water, conceals one of the great geological mysteries of the Sahara: Libyan glass.

A stretch of barchans in the Great Sand Sea

The Great Sand Sea, one of the largest expanses of sand in the world, is roughly the size of Ireland and consists—at least in its central-southern section—of a series of dunes that are sometimes over 100 meters high, arranged in parallel ridges in a northwest-southeast alignment. This immense area, which is 650 kilometers long and 300 km wide on an average, was formed during the Quaternary period with the disintegration of the Nubian sandstone caused by the action of meteoric agents and the prevailing north-northwest winds, which are also responsible for the particular orientation of the series of sand dunes.

These dunes can be as much as 150 km long and are separated from one another by large flat areas one or more kilometers wide, known as interdunal corridors.

The first European to explore this region, which he called "Great Sand Sea", was the German explorer Gerhard Rohlfs. In 1874 Rohlfs crossed it with a caravan of seventeen camels, traveling

The German explorer Gerhard Rohlfs (1831–96)

675 kilometers in thirty-six days.

The Gilf Kebir National Park includes only a tiny portion of the Great Sand Sea, the part situated immediately north of Gilf Kebir, but it is certainly the most interesting part: in fact, it has **Libyan glass** or **LDSG** (*Libyan Desert Silica Glass*), one of the great geological mysteries of the Sahara

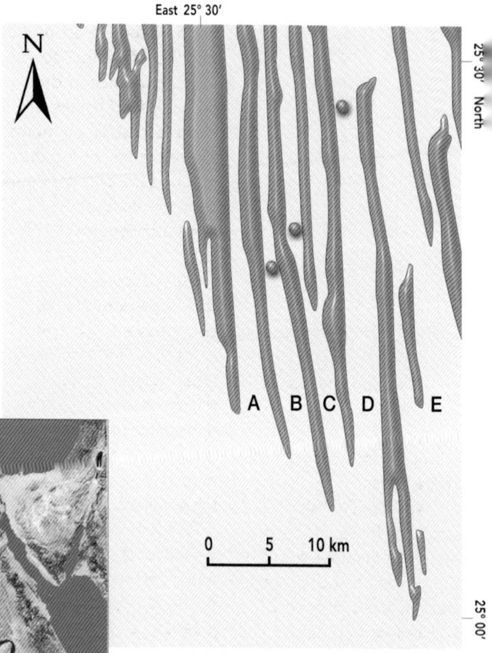

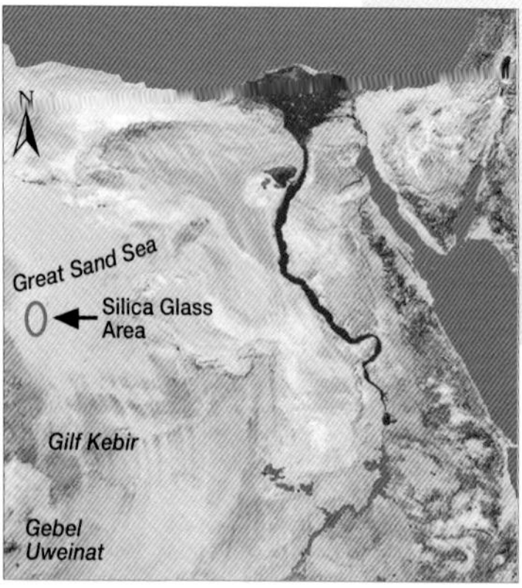

The interdunal corridors in the southern part of the Great Sand Sea (indicated in capital letters),and the sites (in red) where, until few years ago (see box here below), there was a high concentration of Silica glass (map from Bigazzi and De Michele, 1997, and modified)

RESPECT THE SITES

The thoughtless and irresponsible gathering of Silica glass by tourists and merchants has seriously impoverished many sites. Nothing has remained in places where only a few years ago one could admire these splendid 'stones'. Picking up and collecting 'Silica' is severely prohibited and punishable by Egyptian law, and is an actual act of vandalism.

A Silica glass fragment in an interdunal corridor

A Neolithic tool made of Libyan glass or "Silica"

Desert, commonly called **Silica glass**.

It was the English explorer Patrick Clayton who first crossed over the Great Sand Sea from west to east. And on 29 December 1932 he discovered, in an interdunal corridor, many pieces of glass of a pureness that had never before been seen in the rest of the world.

This strange material, which Clayton dubbed 'Libyan glass', is concentrated in a rather small oval area that is about 80 kilometers long and 25 km wide, situated north of the 25th parallel. It has been surmised that this glass is the result of the fusion of the sand due to the impact of a huge meteorite around 28,500,000 years ago.

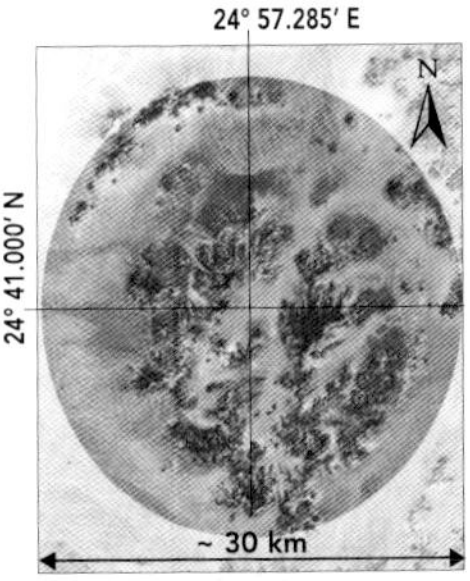

The crater known as Kebira

The presence in the Silica glass of traces of extraterrestrial elements as well as tridymite and cristobalite, two particular forms of quartz whose synthesis requires temperatures over 1400 °C, are points in favor of this hypothesis. But it has a weak point: to date no crater that would testify to the impact made by such a meteorite has been found in an area near that of the Libyan glass.

This led to the theory of the explosion of a cosmic body, probably a comet, at an estimated altitude of 5,000 meters, that gave rise to the immediate fusion of the sand even without any impact on the Earth's surface.

In March 2006, the Egyptian scholar Farouk el-Baz, director of the University of Boston Center for Remote Sensing, announced that by analyzing satellite images he had found a gigantic crater with a 30–kilometer diameter, which he named *Kebira*, at the Egyptian-Libyan border. However, it still must be proved that Kebira is not of volcanic origin but is a crater formed by impact.

The mystery is still far from being solved.

There remains the fact that the prehistoric populations that lived in this area or in the vicinity from 8000 to 5000 BC were well acquainted with Libyan glass and used it as raw material to make utensils (blades, scrapers, and the like).

What is more, the ancient Egyptians also knew of and utilized Libyan glass. Analyses carried out in 1998 on the famous scarab on pharaoh Tutankhamun's pectoral by the Italian geologist Vincenzo De Michele of the Museum of Natural History in Milan have revealed unequivocally that the ancient artisans used Silica glass for this ornament, and not chalcedony, as the discoverer of the young pharaoh's tomb, Howard Carter, had supposed.

The pharaoh Tutankhamun's pectoral with a scarab (Egyptian Museum, Cairo)

BIBLIOGRAPHY

A.A.V.V., *A Concise Report on the Expedition to the Gilf Kebir National Park*, EEAA-Internal Report, Cairo, 2007.

Almásy, L., *Recentes explorations dans le désert lybique (1932-1936)*, Cairo, 1936.

Almásy, L., *Schwimmer in der Wüste*, Leipzig, 1939.

Bagnold, R.A., *Libyan Sands. Travel a Dead World*, London, 1935.

Bubenzer, O., Bolten, A., Darius, F., (edited by), *Atlas of Environmental and Cultural Change in Arid Africa*, in *Africa Praehistorica*, 21, Köln, 2007.

di Caporiacco, L., *Nel cuore del Deserto Libico*, Firenze, 1934.

Clayton, P.A., *A reconaissance of the Gilf Kebir by the late Sir Robert Clayton East Clayton*, in *Geogr. Journal*, 81, 1933.

De Michele, V., (edited by), *Silica'96. Meeting on Libyan Desert Glass and related desert events*, Segrate, 1997.

El-Baz, F., Maxwell, M.A., (edited by), *Desert Landforms in the Southwest Egypt: a basis for comparison with Mars*, Washington, 1982.

Embabi, N.S., *The Geomorphology of Egypt*, Cairo, 2004.

Hassanein Bey, A., *The Lost Oasis*, New York-London, 1925.

Istituto Geografico Militare, *El Auenát*, carta geografica 1:100.000, Firenze, 1933.

Kamal el-Din, H., *L'Exploration du desert Libyque, La Géographie*, 50, 1928

Kröpelin, S., *Palaeoclimatic evidence from Early to Mid-Holocene playas in the Gilf Kebir (Southwest Egypt)*, in *Palaeoecology of Africa*, 18, 1987.

Kuper, R., Kropelin, S., *Climate-Controlled Occupation in the Sahara: Motor of Africa's Evolution*, in *Science*, Vol. 313, 2006.

Le Quellec, J.L., De Flers, P. & Ph., *Du Sahara au Nil. Peintures et gravures d'avant les pharaons*, Paris, 2005.

Linstädter, J., (edited by), *Wadi Bakht - Landschaftsarchäologie einer Siedlungskammer im Gilf Kebir (SW-Ägypten)*, in *Africa Praehistorica*, 18, Köln, 2005.

Monod, Th., Sers, J-F., *Désert libyque*, Paris, 1994.

Rhotert, H., *Libysche Felsbilder*, Darmstadt, 1952.

Schön, W., *Ausgrabungen im Wadi el Akhdar, Gilf Kebir (SW-Agypten)*, Köln, 1996

Said, R., *The Geology of Egypt*, Rotterdam, 1990.

Shaw, W.B.K., *Rock Paintings in the Libyan Desert*, in *Antiquity*, 10, 38, 1936.

Siliotti, A., *The Oases. Egypt Pocket Guide* collection, Cairo, 2007.

Siliotti, A., *Map of the Western Desert: Oases of Egypt*, Cairo, 2007.

Siliotti, A., EEAA, *Map of Gilf Kebir National Park*, Cairo, 2009.

Van Noten, F., *Rock Art of the Jebel Uweinat (Libyan Sahara)*, Graz, 1978.

Zboray, A., *Rock Art of the Libyan Desert*, (DVD), Newbury, 2005.

Negative hands in a cave in the Wadi Sura

PHOTOGRAPH CREDITS

All the photographs in this book are by *Alberto Siliotti*/Archivio Image Service – Geodia except for the following:
Peter Clayton: page 17 above right; *Google™ Earth Pro*: satellite views; *Wally Lama*: pages 17 below right, 34 below right; *Mahmoud Nur el-Din*: page 10 center.